EIGHT NEGRO SPIRITUALS

arranged for S.S.A. (unaccom

JOHN C. PHILLIPS

1 MARY HAD A BA..

19868

4

6

2 YOU GOT A RIGHT

3 NEVER SAID A MUMBALIN' WORD

10

4 THIS TRAIN IS BOUND FOR GLORY

18

this train   Don' pull no-thin' but de right-eous peo-ple,

this train   Don' pull no-thin' but de right-eous peo-ple,

this train   Don' pull no-thin' but de right-eous peo-ple,

28

this train,   this train   don' pull no-thin' but de right-eous peo-ple,

this train,   this train,   no-thin'   but   right-eous peo-ple,

don' pull no-thin' but de right-eous peo-ple,   no-thin'   but   right-eous peo-ple,

poco rall.

30

SOLO   *meno mosso*   *mf ad lib.*

Oh this train   don' pull no-thin' but de right-eous peo-ple,—

this train,—   this train,_____   oh.

this train,—   this train,_____   oh.

this train,—   this train,_____   oh.

meno mosso

32

5 STEAL AWAY TO JESUS

6 LITTLE DAVID, PLAY ON YO' HARP

shout - ed for joy.

shout - ed for joy. *pling pling pling pling* *pling pling pling*

shout - ed for joy. *pling pling pling pling*

28

Lit-tle Dav-id, play on yo' harp, Hal - le - lu, hal - le - lu!

pling *pling pling pling pling* hal - le - lu! *pling pling pling*

pling pling pling pling *pling pling pling pling* hal - le - lu!

32

Lit-tle Dav-id, play on yo' harp, Hal - le - lu!

pling *pling pling pling pling* Hal - le - lu!

pling pling pling pling *pling pling pling pling* Hal - le - lu!

37

7 NOBODY KNOWS DE TROUBLE I SEE, LORD

* This spiritual may be sung once through using either 'Sisters' or 'Brothers', or twice through using one of these the first time and the other on repeat.

8 DRY BONES